Russ and the Gift

Author
Sue Dickson

Illustrated by
Paul Rosado

Page Layout & Design: Jean Hamilton & Paul Rosado

Original Character Design: Norma Portadino • Adapted Character Design: Chip Neville & Jean Hamilton

Modern Curriculum Press, an imprint of Pearson Learning
299 Jefferson Road, P.O. Box 480, Parsippany, NJ 07054
1-800-321-3106 / www.pearsonlearning.com

G H I J K L M N—CJK—05 04 03 02 01

Vocabulary

1. gift

2. golf

3. grass

4. hid

5. left

6. pack

7. Russ

8. top

9. from
(frŭm)

Russ has a gift.
It is in a red box.
The box is not big. 3

Russ tells Mom,
"It is Dad's gift."

4

Russ hid it.

5

6   The bed hid the red box.

SEPTEMBER						
SUNDAY	MONDAY	TUESDAY	WEDNESDAY	THURSDAY	FRIDAY	SATURDAY
	1	2	3	4	5	6
7	8	9	10	11	12	13
14	15	16	17	18	19	20
21	22	23	24	25	26	27
28	29	30				

Russ will give the gift to Dad, but not yet!

7

Dad gets the gift
at last.
Dad is glad.

Mom is glad. 9

Dad held the gift box.

Dad lifts the lid.

Dad held the gift
in his hand.

12

"It is just grand,"
said Dad. 13

"Will it help Dad win?"

14

"Yes, it will," said Russ.

Russ and Dad pack
the golf clubs.

The golf clubs fit in the van.

17

Russ and Dad
went in the van.

19

The van went up the hill.
The golf club is on the left.

21

To the Golf Club

In went Dad.
In went Russ.
22 In went the bag of golf clubs !

23

"Hit it!"
Russ tells Dad.

24

Up and up it went.
It went up fast. 25

It went up the hill.

Is it at the top?

Can Dad get it?
Can Dad hit it?

30 Yes. Dad can get it.

Yes, Dad can hit it.

31

It went in the sand !

32

Can Dad hit it
from the sand ? 33

Yes ! Dad can hit it from the sand.

34

Dad did hit it.

It went in the mud !
Dad is sad.

Dad hit it from the mud.

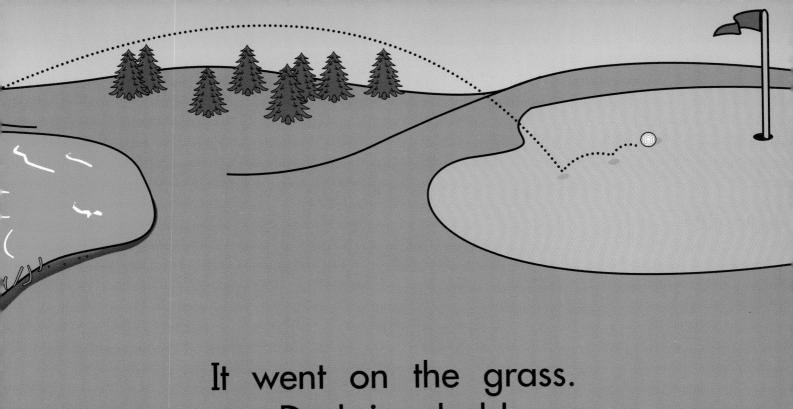

It went on the grass.
Dad is glad !

Dad can hit
it on the grass.

Dad can putt it.

Dad hit it.

42

The flag did not
stop it.

43

Dad can putt it.
It went in the cup.
Dad is glad.

44

45

46   "It is fun," said Dad.

"Yes," said Russ.
Russ is glad.

47

48   Russ' gift is a big hit !